The Tomb of the Unknown Soldier

CORNERSTONES OF FREEDOM

SECOND SERIES

Roger Wachtel

Children's Press®
An Imprint of Scholastic Inc.
New York • Toronto • London • Auckland • Sydney
Mexico City • New Delhi • Hong Kong
Danbury, Connecticut

Photographs © 2003: AP/Wide World Photos: 16, 44 top right; Brown Brothers: 6; Corbis Images: 38, 39 (Bettmann), 36 (Wally McNamee), 7, 44 center (Medford Historical Society Collection), 19, 20, 26; Corbis Sygma/Bill Greenblatt: 30; Folio, Inc./Catherine Karnow: 11; Getty Images: 29, 45 top right (Tim Parker/Reuters), 8, 45 top left (Reuters) 3, 42 (Stefan Zaklin); Hulton|Archive/Getty Images: 12, 13 (Scott Swanson Collection), 14; Library of Congress: 18, 23, 24 (National Photo Company Collection); National Park Service/Don Worth: 4, 44 top left; Photri Inc./TWAchs: bottom cover; Robertstock: 21 (W. Bertsch), 5 (D. Corson), 40, 44 bottom (D. Lada), top cover (J. Patton), 10 (H. Sutton); Superstock, Inc.: 9; The Viesti Collection: 35 (Richard Cummins), 32 (Joe Viesti); TimePix/Leonard McCombe: 27; U.S. Army/Shannon Duckworth: 31, 45 bottom.

Library of Congress Cataloging-in-Publication Data

Wachtel, Roger.
  The Tomb of the Unknown Soldier / Roger Wachtel.
    p. cm. — (Cornerstones of freedom. Second series)
  Summary: A description of the history and characteristics of the national monument known as the Tomb of the Unknown Soldier at Arlington National Cemetary, Arlington, Virginia, which was established after World War I to honor an unidentified soldier from each war.
  Includes bibliographical references and index.
    ISBN-13: 978-0-516-24215-6 (lib.bdg.)   978-0-531-21105-2 (pbk.)
    ISBN-10: 0-516-24215-6 (lib.bdg.)   0-531-21105-3 (pbk.)
    1. Tomb of the Unknowns (Va.)—Juvenile literature. [1. Tomb of the Unknowns (Va.) 2. National monuments.] I. Title. II. Series:
Cornerstones of freedom. Second series.
D675.W2W28 2003
355.1'6'09755295—dc21

                                        2003005621

© 2009 Children's Press, a Division of Scholastic Inc.
All rights reserved. Published simultaneously in Canada.
Printed in China. 62

1 2 3 4 5 6 7 8 9 10 R 18 17 16 15 14 13 12 11 10 09

IN ARLINGTON NATIONAL Cemetery, on a hill overlooking Washington, D.C., is the most honored gravesite in America. While it is surrounded by the burial places of more than 300,000 men and women, many of them famous and highly decorated soldiers, it is the only one with a permanent military guard. Millions of people visit it each year, yet no one even knows who is buried there. As the inscription on the tomb says, "Here rests in honored glory an American Soldier known but to God."

* * * *

Robert E. Lee came to own Arlington House when he married the great-granddaughter of George Washington, Mary Anna Custis. They lived there until 1861, though Lee was frequently away. On May 24, 1861, Union troops occupied the estate. Officers lived in the house while soldiers camped on the grounds.

THE FIRST TOMB OF THE UNKNOWNS

The Tomb of the Unknown Soldier is found at Arlington National Cemetery, the most famous of many American military cemeteries. It is located just across the Potomac River from Washington, D.C. It was established there during the Civil War when General Montgomery Meigs decided to punish Confederate General Robert E. Lee by using his land for the burial of the mounting numbers of Union dead. After the war, the government paid the Lees for the land, but Meigs got his way. The 16,000 soldiers who were buried there guaranteed the Lees would never return.

Although today one must meet certain qualifications to be buried at Arlington, it originally served during the Civil War as a site to bury fallen soldiers whose families were too poor to have their remains shipped home. This often took place without ceremony.

NATIONAL MILITARY CEMETERIES

There are many military cemeteries located in the United States. They are reserved for soldiers, sailors, airmen, and marines who have died in battle and for those who have served with distinction. Their funerals are performed with military honors and the graves are cared for by the U.S. government. Two of the most famous of these are in Arlington, Virginia, and Gettysburg, Pennsylvania. Abraham Lincoln dedicated the Gettysburg cemetery with the Gettysburg Address.

Civil War battles were often furious, and the armies moved on as soon as they were over. Often, old men and boys who were unfit for the army were paid to clean up the battlefields and bury the men. Unless the dead had some identification with them, the gravediggers had no idea who

5

★ ★ ★ ★

they were. Since the battlefields were usually private property, the bodies could not remain there permanently. They had to be **disinterred** and moved. That led to more problems with identification.

In 1866, the unidentified remains of 2,111 soldiers from the battlefields around Washington, D.C., were disinterred and re-buried in a common grave under a stone monument near Arlington House. An inscription on the monument reads, "Beneath this stone repose the bones of two thousand one hundred eleven unknown soldiers gathered

The bloodiest one-day battle in American history took place on September 17, 1862, at Antietam, in northwest Maryland, in the second year of the U.S. Civil War. There were over 23,000 casualties on both sides. For days, the soldiers were left just as they fell.

It normally took a week to bury all the dead after a battle during the Civil War. When soldiers buried their own, they had to do so quickly in order to move on to the next battle. This led to much confusion in identifying the deceased.

after the war from the fields of Bull Run ... Their remains could not be identified, but their names and deaths are recorded in the archives of their country, and its grateful citizens honor them as of their noble army of martyrs. May they rest in peace." They remain there today in the first tomb of unknown soldiers.

WHO CAN BE BURIED AT ARLINGTON?

Members of the military who die on active duty, those who retire from the military, and reservists with long terms of service are eligible for burial at Arlington. Those who have been highly decorated and anyone who has been held as a prisoner of war can also request burial there. There have been notable exceptions made, including personnel killed in the 2001 terrorist attack on the Pentagon and other notable citizens. The spouses of those buried at Arlington may elect to be buried there as well.

On September 12, 2002, a group funeral was held in honor of the victims of the attack on the Pentagon on September 11, 2001. The unidentified remains buried in Arlington Cemetery were in remembrance of all 184 victims.

TO HONOR THOSE WHO NEVER RETURNED

On November 11, 1918, World War I officially ended. It was a war the scope of which the world had never seen. Then referred to as The Great War, it cost thousands of lives— 115,516 from the United States alone. Other countries had their own devastating losses. While many of the dead were returned to their families for burial, many others were never identified. The unidentified men who had lost their lives far from home were most frequently buried in special cemeteries in Europe. Their families never had a chance to properly say goodbye, and the world's governments searched for a way to properly honor those who had given their lives for their countries.

The Battle of Verdun, in World War I, is considered one of the bloodiest in history, with a total of more than 700,000 killed, wounded, or missing on both sides. This blood was shed for a patch of land less than 8 square miles in area in northeast France.

The Arc de Triomphe was commissioned by Napoleon Bonaparte in 1806, but it was not completed until 1836. It was originally intended to honor France's unknown soldiers as well as its generals and major victories from the Revolutionary and Napoleonic periods.

France and England were the first to develop the idea of an unknown soldier. On November 11, 1920, both countries chose and buried one unidentified soldier to represent all those who could not be named. The French placed theirs beneath the Arc de Triomphe in Paris, located at the start of the Champs d'Elysses, Paris' grandest street. The English **interred** theirs in Westminster Abbey, where many of their

A horse-drawn caisson enters Arlington National Cemetery. The tradition of draping the flag over the deceased's casket was adopted from France, where it began during the Napoleonic Wars. In the United States, the flag is always draped so that the blue is at the head and falls over the left shoulder of the deceased.

MILITARY FUNERALS

Military personnel who are buried at Arlington receive military honors at their funerals. Their casket is pulled on a **caisson** or hearse, and draped with an American flag, which is removed and presented to family. A bugler plays "Taps" and a salute is given by a rifle firing team. The higher rank or more honored the serviceman is, the more involved the ceremony. Many funerals are performed at Arlington every day.

most famous artists and leaders are buried. The inscription on his tomb begins: "Beneath this stone rests the body of a British warrior unknown by name or rank." The Italians soon interred their own unknown, and many felt that the United States should as well.

The original proposal for an American tomb was made by Brigadier General William D. Connor, commander of American forces in France. He had heard of the French project and was impressed with the idea. His superiors were not. He was turned down for two reasons. The first was the belief that eventually all the unidentified U.S. soldiers might be identified. The second was that the United States didn't

have any place as appropriately impressive as the Europeans did. New York Congressman Hamilton Fish, Jr., decided there was such a place, and he introduced a resolution in December of 1920 to bring an unidentified serviceman from France and bury him with honor at the Memorial Amphitheater in Arlington National Cemetery.

The resolution passed to begin construction of a simple tomb that would serve as the base for a more appropriate monument at a later date. Congressman Fish hoped the burial would take place on Memorial Day in May of 1921. However, Secretary of War Newton Baker told the committee that the date was too soon. Only about 1,200 soldiers were still unidentified and all of those were still being investigated. If they buried a soldier too soon, he warned, he might later have to be **exhumed** when the government finally learned who he was.

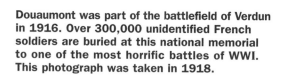

Douaumont was part of the battlefield of Verdun in 1916. Over 300,000 unidentified French soldiers are buried at this national memorial to one of the most horrific battles of WWI. This photograph was taken in 1918.

American troops fire from trenches on the western front in World War I. The Germans were the first to use this method of warfare in an effort to hold onto occupied land in France and Belgium. When the Allies realized these fronts could not be penetrated, they, too, began to build trenches. It was in the trenches that some of the most horrific aspects of modern warfare were introduced—machine guns, gas attacks, and landmines.

THE UNKNOWN SOLDIER OF WORLD WAR I

A presidential election brought a new president and a new secretary of war, but still no unknown soldier. Congressman Fish again pushed for a ceremony to be held on Memorial

* * * *

Day 1921, but the committee finally settled on November 11, 1921, the third anniversary of the war's end. Plans began in earnest for both what form the ceremony would take and how the soldier would be chosen.

In September, the War Department began looking for soldiers buried in France who might represent all those who had been killed and buried anonymously during the war. A body was exhumed from each of the four American military cemeteries in France—Aisne-Maine, Meuse-Argonne, Somme, and St. Mihiel. Each of the four was examined to make sure that he had died of combat wounds and that there were no clues as to the soldier's identity. Then, the bodies were placed in identical caskets and shipping cases.

On October 23, at 3:00 in the afternoon, the four caskets were brought to Chaolons-sur-Marne. There was a large delegation of important officials from the United States military and government as well as France. The caskets were met by a French honor guard and French troops carried the shipping cases to the reception room in the city hall. The caskets were then removed, placed on top of the cases, and covered with American flags. At 10:00 P.M., six American **pallbearers** arrived and began to hold a constant vigil with the French guard.

Making sure the Unknown Soldier was truly unknown was very important. Early the next morning, October 24, 1921, an American officer directed French and American

OVERSEAS MILITARY CEMETERIES

When soldiers, sailors, airmen, and marines die overseas, they are often returned home. Others are buried near where they died. More than 100,000 members of the United States military are buried in American cemeteries located overseas. Some of the best known are in France, near where the D-Day invasion took place, and in Hawaii, where many of the dead from Pearl Harbor and the Pacific Theater of World War II are buried.

On Memorial Day in 1930 at Arlington National Cemetery, Sergeant Edward S. Younger honored the fallen soldier whom he had designated nine years earlier as the symbol for all unknown soldiers. Younger was a highly decorated combat infantryman on duty in Germany when he first chose between the four caskets.

troops to move the caskets. That way no one would have any way of even knowing which cemetery each had come from. The officer then designated Sergeant Edward S. Younger to choose the Unknown Soldier. Originally this was to have been done by an officer, but when American officials learned that the French had given this honor to an enlisted man, they decided to do the same.

The ranking French and American generals each made a short speech honoring the dead. Then Sergeant Younger took a **spray** of roses from a Frenchman who had lost two sons in the war. He walked around the coffins several times before placing the roses on the chosen casket. When later asked why he chose the one he did, he replied, "It was as though something had pulled me. A voice seemed to say to me, 'This is a pal of yours.'" Younger then saluted the fallen soldier, as did the other officials. The pallbearers took the chosen soldier to another room. The other three were then removed to a cemetery near Paris, where they remain today.

Meanwhile, the body of the Unknown Soldier was placed in its special coffin and sealed before witnesses. It was draped with an American flag and the spray of roses. The utmost care had been taken to guarantee that this was indeed an unidentified soldier killed in battle. Equal care guaranteed that he was treated with honor and respect. It was indeed a perfectly executed and moving ceremony.

The Unknown Soldier was taken on a procession through the town the next day. Soldiers, firemen, policemen, and other dignitaries paid tribute as the honor guard took him to a special train for transport to Paris. The guard watched over him all night, and the next day more dignitaries paid him honor and presented him with memorial wreaths. The route to the ship that would transport him to the United

States was lined with bands playing the American national anthem and military marches.

At the pier, the Unknown Soldier was presented with a French Medal of Honor. American Marines presented arms in respect, and the body bearers took him aboard the USS

The body of the Unknown Soldier is carried from the USS *Olympia* at the Navy Yard while America's highest dignitaries of state, army, and navy stand at salute. General John J. Pershing and the Secretary of War, John Weeks, are among those in attendance.

Army Chief of Staff General John Joseph Pershing visited France in 1921, on behalf of President Warren G. Harding, to present the Congressional Medal of Honor to the French Unknown Soldier. Pershing had commanded the U.S. troops in Europe during World War I.

Olympia. Rear Admiral Lloyd Chandler, commander, escorted the casket to the rear of the ship which had been decorated for the occasion. As *Olympia* left the dock, it was escorted by an American destroyer and eight French navy ships. *Olympia* received a 17-gun salute as it set sail for the United States.

THE UNKNOWN SOLDIER COMES HOME

The plans for honoring and burying the Unknown Soldier were just as elaborate, if not more so, as the ceremonies had been in France. On November 9, the *Olympia* sailed up the Potomac River into Washington, receiving military honors from posts along the way. When it docked, the most distinguished military leaders were on hand to

★ ★ ★ ★

President Warren G. Harding places a wreath on the casket of the Unknown Soldier in the rotunda of the Capitol on November 9, 1921. Two days later he would give an emotional speech in honor of the Unknown Soldier and plea for an end to war.

receive the honored dead. Among them were John J. "Black Jack" Pershing, the highly decorated soldier and General of the Armies, as well as the Chief of Naval Operations and the Commandant of the Marine Corps. The Secretaries of War and the Navy attended, along with the 3rd Cavalry, whose job it would be to escort the soldier to the tomb.

As the casket was taken ashore, it was given the honors a full admiral would receive. A band played Chopin's *Funeral*

FAMOUS BURIALS AT ARLINGTON

There are many famous people buried at Arlington National Cemetery. President John F. Kennedy and his brother Robert, both of whom were assassinated, are there. Others include astronaut Gus Grissom, who was killed in a fire aboard *Apollo One*, famous generals Omar Bradley and Jack "Black" Pershing, and polar explorer Admiral Robert E. Byrd. Also in Arlington are boxer Joe Louis and Abner Doubleday, who is often credited with inventing baseball.

The eternal flame that burns at the grave of former president John F. Kennedy was the idea of his widow, Jacqueline Kennedy, inspired by her visit to the memorial of the Unknown Soldier at the Arc de Triomphe in Paris, France, where a similar flame burned.

March and the ship's guns began firing. As he left the ship, a marine bugler played a flourish and the band played the national anthem. The casket was placed on a caisson and the band played "Onward Christian Soldiers." The soldiers and dignitaries then joined in a procession toward the Capitol.

When the procession arrived at the Capitol, the Unknown Soldier was moved into the **rotunda**, where the public could pay its respects. First, however, even more dignitaries visited. This time they were led by President and Mrs. Warren G. Harding, Vice President Calvin Coolidge, the speaker of the House of Representatives, the Chief Justice of the Supreme Court and the Secretary of War, all of whom left flowers. The next day, when the public was allowed to pass by in respect, the crowds were greater than anyone had dreamed. The rotunda was supposed to close at 10:00 P.M., but lines were so long that they were kept open until midnight. By then, 90,000 men and women had passed by to honor the Unknown Soldier.

FINALLY LAID TO REST

The bearers who took the Unknown Soldier to Arlington were all non-commissioned officers. Like everything else done that day, they were chosen so that the symbolism and ceremony of the day would pay due respect to those Americans who had lost their lives in battle. The procession included clergy, the president and vice president, all the military leadership in the country, members of Congress and the Supreme Court, and officials from all over the

The original funeral procession for the first Unknown Soldier commences from the steps of the U.S. Capitol, November 11, 1921. It would take over three hours for the procession to reach Arlington National Cemetery, where over 5,000 attendees would observe the ceremony from the Memorial Amphitheater.

United States. Also in the column was a special group of soldiers who had received the Medal of Honor.

The procession left the Capitol at 8:00 A.M. on November 11, 1921. As it did, an artillery battery began firing once every minute. They would continue to do so throughout the ceremonies, except for a two-minute silence at noon. The

The Unknown Soldier is committed to his final resting place in Arlington National Cemetery. The bottom of the crypt had been lined with a layer of soil from France, where the deceased had first been buried.

procession passed through Washington toward the cemetery for more than three hours, finally arriving at the amphitheater at about 11:40.

The ceremony began in earnest after the moment of silence at noon. The assembled sang "America," and President Harding made an address paying tribute to the soldier and pleading for an end to war. He then placed a Distinguished

24

Service Cross and Medal of Honor on the casket. Foreign dignitaries also bestowed honors on the soldier, many of which had never been given to a soldier of a foreign nation before. Readings from the Bible and hymns followed. "Nearer My God to Thee" closed the ceremony.

The procession then moved to the tomb itself. The clergy read the burial service and Congressman Fish, the man who had initiated the legislation making way for the Tomb of the Unknown Soldier, placed a wreath on the casket. Plenty Coups, Chief of the Crow Nation representing Native Americans, placed his war bonnet on the tomb. The artillery battery fired three shots as the casket was lowered into the tomb, the bottom of which was covered with soil from France. A bugler played "Taps," and the battery fired a twenty-one-gun salute to honor the Unknown Soldier of World War I.

THE UNKNOWNS OF WORLD WAR II AND KOREA

The World War I Unknown Soldier lay alone for years before the government decided to add more fallen men to the tomb. Meanwhile, changes were made to the tomb's exterior.

In 1932, a large **sarcophagus**, which had been called for but not funded in the original legislation, was added. The marble's engravings hold much symbolism: On the east side are three figures which represent the three allies from World War I. They also represent victory, valor, and peace. The peace figure has a palm branch to reward the devotion and sacrifice that, with courage, "make the cause of righteousness triumphant." The other sides each have

★ ★ ★ ★

THE MEDAL OF HONOR

The Medal of Honor is the United States' highest military decoration. It is awarded for soldiers who perform acts of bravery "above and beyond the call of duty." Frequently these acts put the recipients' life in danger, and many are given to soldiers who died saving others' lives. They are also awarded to U.S. Unknown Soldiers. The only Medals of Honor ever given to foreign soldiers were awarded to other countries' unknowns.

Family members are not allowed onboard military vessels for the burials at sea of a fallen member of the armed forces. However, the next of kin is quickly contacted with information about the ceremony. Here, the ceremony is performed in November 1943 for two sailors who were aboard an aircraft carrier torpedoed by a Japanese submarine.

three inverted wreaths. The one facing the amphitheater bears the famous inscription, "Here rests in honored glory an American Soldier known but to God."

In 1956, President Dwight Eisenhower signed a bill to honor unknown soldiers from World War II and Korea just as they had been honored for World War I. He had been the commanding general of Allied troops in World War II, so it seemed appropriate that he would oversee these ceremonies. These soldiers were selected and honored much the same

26

Sergeant Ned Lyle
chooses the Korean
Unknown Soldier in
May 1958 in Hawaii. The
Korean conflict ended
on July 27, 1953, after
37 months of fighting
and 3 million casualties.

way as the World War I unknown had been. The official ceremonies occurred in 1958.

The World War II unknown was selected from soldiers exhumed from cemeteries in Europe and the Pacific. They were placed in identical caskets aboard the USS *Canberra*, and Navy Hospitalman 1ˢᵗ Class William Charette, the Navy's only active duty Medal of Honor recipient, chose one for interment at Arlington. The other was given a burial at sea with full honors.

Four Korean War unknowns were disinterred from a military cemetery in Hawaii. Army Master Sergeant Ned Lyle chose the soldier to be interred. Both the World War II and Korean caskets arrived in Washington on May 28, 1958, and lay in the rotunda until May 30. On that day, they were carried to Arlington National Cemetery on caissons just as their World War I comrade had been. There, President Eisenhower awarded them the Medal of Honor and they were interred on the plaza next to the sarcophagus.

BAKER'S FEARS REALIZED— THE VIETNAM UNKNOWN

In 1920, Secretary of War Newton Baker warned that choosing an unknown soldier too soon would be a mistake. He was afraid that after the unknown had been buried, army investigators would discover his identity and he would have to be exhumed. While it didn't happen then, it did 78 years later.

Advances in medicine and record keeping made finding an unknown soldier from the Vietnam War more difficult than it had been for the other wars. Though Congress called for a search for a Vietnam unknown in 1973, it wasn't until 1984, some nine years after the official end of the war, that Sergeant Major and Medal of Honor recipient Alan Jay Kellogg, Jr., designated the Vietnam unknown.

President and Mrs. Ronald Reagan and many Vietnam veterans attended ceremonies in Arlington National Cemetery on Memorial Day, May 28, 1984. As tradition dictated, the president presided over the ceremonies and awarded the Medal of Honor to the Unknown Soldier and accepted the interment flag as honorary next of kin. At that point, however, the Vietnam unknown's experience became radically different than the others.

Lieutenant Michael J. Blassie's fighter jet was shot down on May 11, 1972, by North Vietnamese anti-aircraft guns. Because the area was heavily controlled by enemy forces, no recovery attempts could be immediately launched. However, eyewitness accounts eventually led to Blassie's identification.

In 1994, a highly decorated Vietnam veteran named Ted Sampley began researching the circumstances around the time and place of death of the soldier whose remains were interred as the Vietnam unknown. He had been declared unknown because of the condition of his body and the fact that several kinds of aircraft had crashed in that area. There

★ ★ ★ ★

DNA TESTING

DNA (deoxyribonucleic acid) is a set of chemical strands that include genetic material. In short, it is the material that makes humans unique from one another. In recent years, scientists have been able to extract and "look" at DNA. Each person's DNA is different, so it can be used to identify people, even after death. Since humans share a large part of their DNA with their close relatives, DNA can be matched to find out if people are related.

Jean Blassie poses with a photo of her son, Lieutenant Michael J. Blassie. For 26 years he was considered MIA before his remains were identified as the Vietnam unknown. Jean, who could not speak of her missing son for years, said, "In my heart I always knew he was gone, but there's always that doubt."

seemed to be too many possibilities to make a credible guess of the man's identity as far as the military was concerned.

Sampley, however, used evidence that had been found nearby to determine that the body was that of a pilot of a single seat plane. That meant it was probably Lt. Michael J. Blassie. He published his information, which was reprinted by a national news organization. Blassie's family soon learned of the news and asked the Secretary of Defense to exhume the body and test its DNA to make a positive determination. In 1998, the body was positively identified as Lt. Blassie. He was returned to his family in St. Louis and then buried near his childhood home.

The question then was what to do with the Vietnam tomb. After much debate, the Department of Defense determined that it was unlikely that another soldier would ever

The removal of the Vietnam unknown was an emotional moment for the guards at Arlington, who are honored to protect the unknowns year-round, throughout any weather. In the words of one sentinel, "They gave their identities and their lives for their country and ask for nothing in return."

be truly unknown. Science has simply advanced so far that virtually any body can be identified. Instead, government officials decided to leave the tomb empty and dedicate a new inscription to honor those soldiers who are never found. They are declared "missing in action," and the uncertainty of that designation is very hard for loved ones left behind. For those soldiers and their families, the inscription now reads, "Honoring and Keeping Faith With America's Missing Servicemen." It was dedicated in 1999.

The U.S. Army Drill Team is one of the 3rd Infantry's specialty units. They perform numerous breathtaking drills to the delight of proud Americans, foreign dignitaries, and heads of state. To achieve perfection with their intricate maneuvers, they must practice constantly.

THE OLD GUARD

To most people who visit the Tomb of the Unknown Soldier, the most enduring image is the guards who watch it 24 hours a day. They stand in perfect military posture, ensuring that the men laid to rest there will never be disturbed. Visitors are often surprised to learn, then, that the tomb was completely unguarded from 1921 to 1925. In 1925, a civilian guard was hired to watch the tomb during the day, but it was left unattended at night. It wasn't until March 25, 1926, that a permanent armed guard was posted to the tomb "to prevent any desecration or disrespect." Now, only army personnel can be assigned to that duty. The army was so honored because it is the oldest of the service branches.

For several years, the duty moved from unit to unit, until 1946 when it was permanently assigned to the 3rd U.S. Infantry. The 3rd U.S. Infantry is an old and highly decorated unit of the U.S. Army established in 1784. It is referred to as the Old Guard. General Winfield Scott, impressed with the 3rd Infantry's fierce fighting, gave the unit the nickname during a victory parade during the Mexican War. People who have seen the Old Guard **sentinels** at the Tomb of the Unknowns have been just as impressed.

In addition to providing sentinels for the unknowns, the Old Guard performs other military ceremonies in and around Washington, D.C. That means more than 6,000 ceremonies a year, but the unit is by no means just a ceremonial one. It also provides military security to the nation's capital during any national emergency. In fact,

33

members of the 3ʳᵈ Infantry were instrumental in securing safety in Washington, D.C., on September 11, 2001, when the Pentagon was attacked by terrorists. It is based at Fort Myer, which is next to Arlington National Cemetery.

The Old Guard is known for two distinguishing characteristics. Every Old Guardsman wears a black and tan "buff strap" on his left shoulder. It is supposed to represent the knapsack strap that members of the 3ʳᵈ Infantry wore in the 1800s. They also march in parades with fixed **bayonets** on their rifles. This honor commemorates a Mexican War battle when the 3ʳᵈ routed Mexican troops with a bayonet charge. Only the Old Guard has this honor.

THE SILENT SENTINELS

Guarding the Tomb of the Unknown Soldiers is extremely stressful, difficult duty. The soldiers who do so have to meet extremely high standards and maintain them for their entire period of service. It's not for everyone. In fact, it's not for most people—all the guards are volunteer. If they later find the duty is too difficult, they can transfer to other 3ʳᵈ Infantry duty, no questions asked.

If a soldier wants to be a guard for the Tomb, or, sentinel, he must meet several requirements. These are so exacting that more than 80 percent of the applicants do not make it through the interview process. He must have a perfect military record and no criminal record. He must be in excellent physical condition and at least five feet ten inches tall. He must submit to intensive interviews with the sergeant of

Among the various medals awarded for heroic service in the U.S. military is the Purple Heart (far left), established by General George Washington during the Revolutionary War.

the guard, and officers of the 3rd Infantry. The interviews attempt to determine why he wants to be a guard and that his reasons support and respect the importance of that duty. The interviewers ascertain that the soldiers know how difficult the duty is. Soldiers must serve as sentinels for at

Mourners line the streets of Washington in late November 1963 to get a glimpse of the horse-drawn caisson carrying the body of President John F. Kennedy, who had been assassinated several days earlier. The horse being led behind the caisson bears an empty saddle. This is a tradition to show that the "warrior" will never ride again.

least two years. As a former sentinel once said, "You have to be perfect."

Once a soldier is selected for guard duty, an intensive period of training begins. The months of training and practicing move each soldier toward the perfection every one of them is expected to achieve. Physical and mental fitness are

* * * *

stressed, and each is expected to become an expert on Arlington National Cemetery and the Tomb of the Unknown Soldier. They are regularly reviewed and tested, inspected and tested again. When they begin their period of duty, the reviews continue regularly to guarantee perfection. Guards are evaluated on uniform, posture, arm swing, heel clicks, timing, and walk, among other things. The intensity of these evaluations is one of the reasons guards serve such a short time.

All Sentinels of the Tomb wear a special insignia. It is a badge with a likeness of the Tomb surrounded by a laurel leaf. Underneath are the words, "Honor Guard." Anyone serving as sentinel for at least nine months is entitled to wear the badge permanently. The guards wear the Army Dress Blue uniforms while on duty. As they march back and forth protecting the Tomb, guards carry their rifles on the shoulder closest to the visitor, as a gesture of protecting the Tomb against any threat.

Even the guard's walk is steeped in symbolism. He crosses back and forth in front of the Tomb on a 63-foot rubber mat (placed there to prevent wear). He must cross in exactly 21 steps. At the end, he pauses 21 seconds, turns, pauses 21 more seconds, and retraces his 21 steps. Each time he stops, he performs a sharp click of his heels. Twenty-one is an honored number symbolic of the highest salute used in military ceremonies.

LAYING WREATHS AT THE TOMB OF THE UNKNOWNS

Many individuals and groups wish to lay a wreath at the Tomb of the Unknown Soldier to honor him and what the Tomb represents. To do so they must request and receive permission well in advance. They schedule their visit to the Tomb and are allowed, with the assistance of Tomb guards, to take part in a brief ceremony. About 2,000 wreaths are laid each year, including Veterans' and Memorial Day ceremonies, usually involving the president.

37

Members of the Kennedy family mourn at Robert F. Kennedy's funeral in Arlington National Cemetery on June 8, 1968. He had served as attorney general under his brother, President John F. Kennedy, before becoming a senator representing New York. He was slain on June 5, 1968, during his campaign for presidency.

Almost all guard activities are performed in silence. If someone attempts to enter the restricted area around the Tomb, for instance, the guard will stop and bring his rifle in front of him as a warning. If that fails, only then will he speak a warning.

Every hour, or half hour in the summer, the guard is relieved and replaced in a short ceremony that includes inspection of the guards' uniforms and weapons. This is performed in almost total silence by an officer of the guard. At night, the guard changes every two hours.

The Changing of the Guard is one of the military's proudest traditions. The ceremony at the Tomb of the Unknown Soldier happens more frequently in the summertime to give visitors an opportunity to witness the event during daylight hours.

While their watch is largely symbolic, occasionally people do stray into the restricted area and have to be warned off by the guard. In 1984, a disturbed civilian briefly took one of the sentinels hostage at gunpoint. In that instance, off duty guards disarmed him from behind and no one was injured.

The sentinels of the Tomb of the Unknown Soldier understand better than anyone the importance of their duty and the sacred nature of the place they protect. So that they never forget, one of their first obligations is to learn the Sentinels' Creed:

> *My dedication to this sacred duty is total and wholehearted.*
>
> *In the responsibility bestowed on me never will I falter.*
>
> *And with dignity and perseverance my standard will remain perfection.*
>
> *Through the years of diligence and praise and the discomfort of the elements,*
>
> *I will walk my tour in humble reverence to the best of my ability.*
>
> *It is he who commands the respect I protect.*
>
> *His bravery that made us so proud.*
>
> *Surrounded by well meaning crowds by day alone in the thoughtful peace of night,*
>
> *this soldier will in honored glory rest under my eternal vigilance.*

★ ★ ★ ★

When wars are fought, young men die. Many times they die alone and anonymously far from their homes. The Tomb of the Unknown Soldier recognizes this ultimate sacrifice on what is probably the most sacred ground in the United States. Whether it honors the soldiers who died and went unidentified, those who never came home, or the loved ones who miss their sons and daughters so terribly, the Tomb of the Unknown Soldier will ever remain one of our most important places of remembrance.

Glossary

bayonets—knives adapted to fit on the end of rifles to
be used in close combat

caisson—a horse-drawn vehicle, formerly used to carry
ammunition. Used symbolically in military funeral
to bear a soldier's body

disinterred—removed from a grave or tomb

exhumed—dug up

interred—placed in a grave or tomb for burial

pallbearer—one who carries a casket during funeral
ceremonies

rotunda—an area underneath the domed part of
a building

sarcophagus—a stone coffin

sentinel—one who keeps watch, usually in the military

spray—a bouquet of flowers

Timeline: The Tomb of

1778 | 1861 | 1864 | 1866 | 1919 | 1920

John Parke Custis buys the land that will eventually become Arlington National Cemetery and Fort Myer Military Reservation.

1861
Union troops seize Arlington House.

JUNE 15
General Montgomery Meigs proposes the Arlington House property as the site of the next military cemetery.

MAY 13
Private William Christman is the first soldier buried at what would become Arlington National Cemetery.

1866
The remains of 2,111 union soldiers are buried in a common grave as "unknown soldiers."

OCTOBER 29
General William D. Connor proposes the burial of an unknown soldier, similar to the ones being proposed in France and England. His idea is rejected.

DECEMBER 21
Congressman Hamilton Fish, Jr., introduces legislation calling for the tomb of an unknown soldier killed in action in France. The measure is approved the following March.

the Unknown Soldier

1921 | 1932 | 1958 | 1984 | 1998 | 1999

OCTOBER 24
Sergeant Edward S. Younger selects a soldier from four exhumed from American military cemeteries in France, to serve as the Unknown Soldier.

NOVEMBER 11
The Unknown Soldier is interred in official ceremonies at Arlington National Cemetery.

1932
A large sarcophagus is placed on the Tomb of the Unknown Soldier, completing the project called for in the original 1920 legislation.

1958 — MAY 30
Unknown soldiers from World War II and Korean conflict are laid to rest on the plaza next to the World War I soldier.

1984 — MAY 28
An unknown soldier from the Vietnam War is laid to rest with his comrades from previous wars.

1998
After investigation, the Vietnam unknown is exhumed and positively identified as Lt. Michael Blassie. His remains are returned to his family for interment near his home.

1999
A new inscription honoring missing servicemen is dedicated on what was the Vietnam Unknown Tomb. Decision is to leave the Tomb permanently and symbolically empty.

To Find Out More

BOOKS AND JOURNALS

Bigler, Philip. *In Honored Glory, Arlington National Cemetery: The Final Post*. Vandameer, New York: 1999.

Dieterle, Lorraine. *Arlington National Cemetery: A Nation's Story Carved in Stone*. Pomegranate Books, New York: 2001.

Peters, James Edward. *Arlington National Cemetery: Shrine to America's Heroes*. Woodbine House, Bethesda, MD: 2000.

Temple, Bob. *Arlington National Cemetery: Where Heroes Rest*. Child's World, Chanhassen, MD: 2000.

ONLINE SITES

Arlington National Cemetery: Tomb of the Unknowns. The official website of Arlington National Cemetery with sections on the Tomb of the Unknowns.
http://www.arlingtoncemetery.com/tombofun.htm

Society of the Honor Guard of the Tomb of the Unknown Soldier. The official website of the men who have guarded the tombs.
http://www.tombguard.org/

Index

About the Author

Roger Wachtel has been an educator for 17 years, first as a high school English teacher, then as a university instructor. He is now the writing specialist for the Peru Community Schools in Peru, Indiana. He was born in New Jersey, went to high school in Belgium, and now lives in Westfield, Indiana. He is married to Jeanette and has three sons, Thomas, Ben, and Josh. He has a Master's degree in English Education from Butler University. In his spare time, he reads and writes, follows the New York Mets passionately, and goes to automobile races with his sons and brothers. Roger has written three other books for the Cornerstones of Freedom series, *Medal of Honor*, *Old Ironsides*, and *The Donner Party*.